If You're Riding a Horse and It Dies, Get Off

by Jim Grant and
Char Forsten

Illustrated by Nathan Bundy

Crystal Springs
BOOKS

Published by
Crystal Springs Books • Peterborough, New Hampshire
1-800-321-0401

If You're Riding a Horse and It Dies, Get Off
by Jim Grant and Char Forsten

Published by:
Crystal Springs Books
10 Sharon Road
PO Box 500
Peterborough, NH 03458

1-800-321-0401
www.crystalsprings.com
www.sde.com

Illustrations by Nathan Bundy

ISBN: 1-884548-25-3

Dedication

About the Illustrator

If You're Riding a Horse and It Dies, Get Off may be Nate Bundy's first illustrated book, but this first-year college student has been drawing ever since he could hold a crayon. While Nate is new to the world of book illustration, he has made numerous contributions as a member of the Crystal Springs Books Graphic Arts Department. Nate is a film major at Keene State College located in Keene, NH.

About This Book

Years ago a tractor trailer truck got stuck while heading into a Boston tunnel. City officials were confounded as to how they were going to move it. Some suggested they hire a blasting crew to remove part of the tunnel; others suggested that the roof of the truck and trailer be sawed off. Meanwhile, traffic was piling up and patience was wearing thin. Finally, a child stepped forward and suggested they let some air out of the truck tires and back it out to a nearby exit ramp. Needless to say, it worked—the truck was removed and traffic was soon flowing smoothly.

What does this have to do with the story you are about to read? School systems and businesses alike are constantly barraged with suggestions from well-intentioned people on how to make a program or initiative work when there is absolutely no hope for its success. The best alternative, as suggested in this story, is to take a fresh look at the problem and design a plan that makes sense.

Do you think a bigger whip would help?

Let's visit some schools that are successfully riding dead horses.

Has anyone thought of using
an electric prod?

Let's try a more experienced rider.

Let's assemble a committee
to study dead horses.

I think we should raise the standards
for riding dead horses.

I think testing the horse would help.

I think we should evaluate the
horse's reputation.

What about implementing an Individual Equestrian Plan (IEP)?

Why don't we try adding an
additional saddle.

Let's try team riding.

We will categorically deny there is anything wrong with the horse.

The basic problem is the horse's parents-poor breeding!

Let's try throwing more money
at the problem.

I think we should give the rider
a competency test.

What I think is needed is
federal assistance.

I know what to do! If you're riding a horse
and it dies, get off the horse . . .

and try something new.

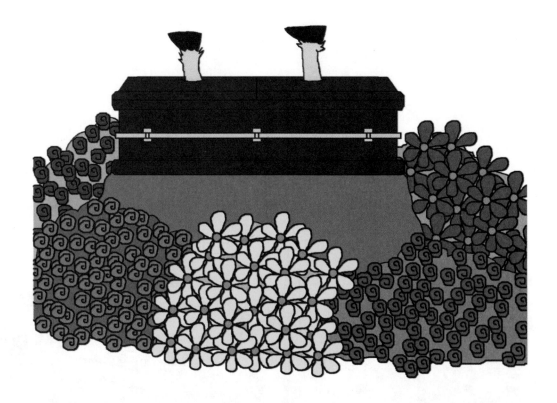

If you were riding a horse and it died, what would you do? Ancient wisdom advises the rider to dismount and find a better mode of transportation, whether it be another horse or something entirely different. Unfortunately, too often people try to revive the dead horse with well-intentioned yet unrealistic solutions.

Today, school systems nationwide are continuing to ride their own version of "the dead horse." Most affected by this practice are teachers and students who suffer under reforms that often just do not make sense. The message presented in this book is our attempt to emphasize the importance and necessity of applying common sense practices to present-day and future school reform. So if you're attempting to ride a dead horse, or if you know someone else who is attempting to ride a dead horse, our best advice is to get off and find something that works.